THE WARM HUG BOOK

THE WARM HUG BOOK

WILLIAM L. COLEMAN

BETHANY HOUSE PUBLISHERS
MINNEAPOLIS, MINNESOTA 55438
A Division of Bethany Fellowship, Inc.

Scripture quotations, unless otherwise marked, are taken from *The Living Bible*, copyright 1971 by Tyndale House Publishers, Wheaton, IL. Used by permission.

Photos by Jon Dugan, Dick Easterday, Gary Johnson and Fred Renich

Published by Bethany House Publishers
A Division of Bethany Fellowship, Inc.
6820 Auto Club Road, Minneapolis, MN 55438

Printed in the United States of America

Library of Congress Cataloging in Publication Data

Coleman, William L.
  The warm hug book.

  Summary: A collection of devotions in verse, with related Bible verses, exploring the importance of happy hugs, welcome-home hugs, father-climbing, and other kinds of healthy physical contact.
    1. Children—Prayer-books and devotions—English.
  2. Hugging—Juvenile literature.   [1. Prayer books and devotions.
  2. Hugging] I. Easterday, Dick, ill.
  II. Title.

BV4870.C6395   1985   242'.62   85-6175
ISBN 0-87123-794-6

About the Author

BILL COLEMAN has written several bestselling devotional books for this age group (three to seven) besides his very popular family devotional books for older children and teens. His experience as a pastor, a father and a writer help to give him his special relationship with children. He and his family make their home in Aurora, Nebraska.

Also in This Series

Contents

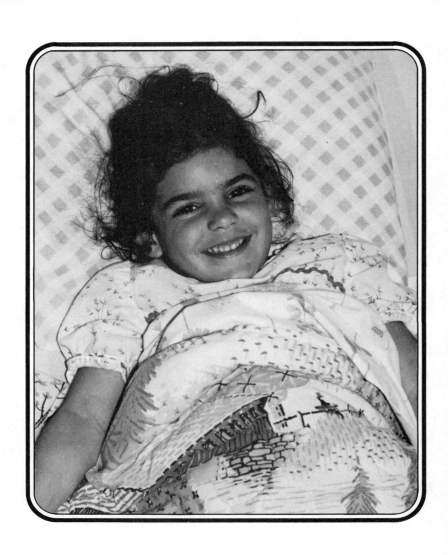

Keep in Touch

Hugging and touching are healthy activities we each need. *Holding* our children helps create a bond that few other actions can. If you want to make children feel good about themselves, be sure to give them wholesome physical contact.

A happy hug a day will help make your child feel important, wanted and special. Most likely it will make *you* feel good, too!

Unfortunately, physical contact has been abused and given a bad name by some. That is no reason to give it up. Touching is too vital to abandon. We meet many children and adults who long to be held.

Far better that we teach children the difference between acceptance and harmful touching than to avoid it altogether. We have included some chapters in this book to help discuss dangerous touching. You are a smart parent for opening this subject to your child.

I know you will be glad you have promoted physical contact in the right context. God bless you as you express love and tenderness to the children in your family.

Bill Coleman
Aurora, Nebraska

When to Hug Someone

People enjoy hugs
Just about anytime.

People like to be hugged
At ballgames,
At breakfast,
At parades
And at the zoo.

People like to be hugged
On mountaintops,
In rowboats,
At rodeos,
In the rain
And at birthday parties.

People like to be hugged
On sleighs,
In airplanes,
In mud puddles,
On trains
And on roller coasters.

People like to be hugged
Under trees,
In fields,
On elevators,
On motorcycles
And on buses.

But one of the best times
To hug someone
Is just before you go
To sleep.

You are going to wiggle
Under the covers
And snuggle your head
Into your pillow.

Before you do that, you might
Want to hug someone.
Maybe your mother
Or your father
Or another person
Who takes care of you
Would be the best person to hug.

Sometimes
Bedtime is the best time
To give someone
A good hug.

God likes to see
You give hugs.

"A time to hug." (Eccles. 3:5)

A Happy Hug

Have you ever felt so good
That you wanted to grab someone
And give him a huge hug?

Maybe you received a special present
For your birthday
And you were so happy
You threw your arms
Around your parents.

Maybe you were playing a game
And your team won,
So you hugged the person
Next to you.

There are lots of good ways
To show you are happy.
Some people jump up and down.
Some people smile big and wide.
Some people shake hands.

But others find a friend
Or they find a parent
Or they find a brother
Or a sister
And they hug.

Happiness is so much fun,
It is often hard
To keep it all inside.

A warm, tight hug
Tells people
Just how good we feel.

When we follow God
And believe Him,
We have many reasons
To be happy.

If you know that
God loves you,
You can give your parents
A big
Happy hug.

**"God blesses those who obey him; happy
the man who puts his trust in the Lord."
(Prov. 16:20)**

One Arm or Two?

There are lots of good ways
To hug.
You can hug someone
With two arms or
With one.

A two-arm hug is good
Because
Two arms give you strength.

You can hold someone
With both arms
And squeeze him firmly
Until he smiles.

A good two-arm hug
Lets someone hug you back
At the same time.

Most people use the two-arm hug
Most of the time.

However, a one-arm hug
Is just as important
And a one-arm hug can be used
When you can't use two arms.

If you are carrying something
Like a doll or a toy
In one hand,

You can still hug someone
With your other arm.

If you have a candy bar
Or an ice cream cone
In one hand,
You can still hug someone
With your other arm.

And what if you are
Standing with two friends,
One on each side of you?
You can hug both of them
With one arm for
Each friend.

There are lots of good ways
To hug.
Some of the best ways are
With two arms or
With one arm.

God doesn't have physical arms
Like you have.
But God is so close to you,
It seems like
He is hugging you.

Relax for a minute
And pretend that
You can feel
God hugging you.

**"The eternal God is your Refuge, and
underneath are the everlasting arms."
(Deut. 33:27)**

A Hand to Squeeze

We can't always
Hug each other.
We can't hug while
We are doing dishes.

We can't hug while
We are cleaning the car.

Sometimes it is easier
To hold hands than
To hug.

We often hold hands
With our mother or father
When we go for walks.

We often hold hands
When we help
Our brother or sister
Cross the street.

When you were little
And just learning
To walk,
You probably held just
One of your parents'
Fingers.

You and I can't see God,
But He walks beside us
As if He were holding
Our hand.

Day or night,
Home or school,
Car or plane,
City or country,
Awake or asleep,
God is always there.

Just as if He were
Holding your hand.

Go ahead!
You can squeeze
God's hand.

**"I am holding you by your right hand—I,
the Lord your God—and I say to you, Don't
be afraid; I am here to help you."
(Isa. 41:13)**

Hugging Babies

Do you have
A baby brother
Or a baby sister
At your house?

Does someone bring a baby
To your house
To visit once in a while?

Babies are cute and tiny
And soft and cuddly.
Almost everyone likes to
Hold a little baby.

Do you ever get to hold
The baby?
Do you sit in a chair
Or on a couch
And let the baby rest
In your arms?

It makes you feel special
And grown-up to
Hold a baby.

If you are old enough
To hold a baby,
You must be big enough
To hold it correctly.

How do you
Hold a baby carefully?

Well, you never squeeze it
Very hard and
You never hug it
Too tightly.

It makes you feel special
And grown-up to
Hold a baby.

**"Simeon . . . took the child in his arms,
praising God." (Luke 2:28)**

The Sneaky Surprise

Do you like to surprise people?
Do you ever hide behind a door
And when someone walks past,
Jump out and yell, "Boo!"?

Have you ever put a toy
Under someone's pillow to surprise him?

Another way to surprise people
Is to walk up quietly
And give them a
Sneaky hug.

If you are careful, they will not
See you coming.
If you step quietly, they will not
Hear you coming.

But they will have a
Happy surprise
When they are squeezed by a
Sneaky hug.

Be careful to make sure
The person is not carrying
Anything hot or
Anything that
Will spill.

Tiptoe up behind him
And wrap your arms

Around his leg and say,
"Sneaky hug!"

If you do it a few times,
You'd better watch out
Because someone might come up behind you
And give you a
"Sneaky hug!"

**"Let us outdo each other in being helpful
and kind to each other and in doing good."
(Heb. 10:24)**

Your Furry Friends

Do you have any stuffed animals
On your bed or on a shelf?
Do you like to hold them tightly
Or play games with them?

It feels good to hug a furry animal.
Maybe yours has a cute nose
Or round white eyes.

Some furry animals become your friends
For years and years.
My daughter, Mary,
Has a stuffed dog named Fred.
Her grandfather gave it to her
When she was two years old.
When Mary left for college,
She took Fred with her
To college.

Do you like to sleep with
Your stuffed, furry friend?
Do you ever like to talk
To your friend after the light
Is turned off?
That's a lot of fun.

Do you hold your furry friend
And go to sleep with it
Still in your arms?
That's a lot of fun.

Stuffed animals feel good.
Stuffed animals feel warm.
Stuffed animals feel fuzzy.

When you go to sleep tonight,
Give your furry animal
An extra tight hug.
It is nice to have a furry friend around.

When You Need to Feel Better

Have you ever had a cold
And your head was hot
And your nose was running
And you felt terrible?

Almost all of us have felt
That way,
Sometime.

When you feel terrible,
It is nice if someone
Wraps his arms
Around you and
Gives you a hug.

Have you ever lost a toy,
A special, favorite toy,
And couldn't find it anywhere?
Did you feel terrible?

Maybe all of us have felt
That way,
Sometime.

When you feel terrible,
It is nice if someone
Wraps his arms
Around you
And gives you a hug.

Sometimes you feel sad.
You don't want to do *anything*.
You let your head drop
And you stare at the floor.

You might feel better
If someone would
Give you a big hug.

Sometimes your parents
Feel terrible, too.
You can see it
In their faces.
You can hear it
In their voices.

Maybe all of us have felt
That way,
Sometime.

You can help them
Feel a little better
If you give them
A gentle hug
And a warm
"I love you."

**"Share each other's troubles and problems,
and so obey our Lord's command."
(Gal. 6:2)**

Good Hugs Never Hurt

Hugs are nice because
They are gentle and
They make you feel good.

If a hug were so hard
It hurt the person,
A hug would not be
Any fun.

If you were squeezed
So hard
It made you yell,
A hug would not be
Any fun.

If you were hugged
So hard
It made you cry,
A hug would not be
Any fun.

Good hugs are tight enough
So the person can feel them,
But never so tight that
They would hurt someone.

A good hugger is
A gentle hugger.

**"The wisdom that comes from heaven is
. . . full of quiet gentleness." (James 3:17)**

Riding on Shoulders

One of the best ways
To get around
Is to ride on someone's
Tall shoulders.

Riding on shoulders
Gives you a way to
See all around
The yard
Or all the way
Down the street.

It makes you feel
Eight feet tall.

When you ride on
Someone's shoulders,
You put one leg
On each shoulder
And you have
A comfortable seat.

For a steering wheel,
You hold on to
The person's head.

If you aren't careful,
You might put your hands
Over his eyes
And he won't be able
To see.

If you go someplace
That is crowded
And you can't see,
You can get up
On someone's shoulders
And look over
The crowd.

It makes you happy
To have some
Tall shoulders
To sit on.

While you are
Up high,
Be sure to
Give a hug.

"The beloved of the Lord shall dwell in safety by him; and the Lord shall cover him all the day long, and he shall dwell between his shoulders." (Deut. 33:12, KJV)

Holding Hands

Jim was going across
A busy highway with
His father.
Before they started across,
Jim's father said,
"Take my hand, Jim."

Jim smiled
And put his hand
Into his father's hand.

It feels good to hold
Your parent's hand.
Holding hands makes
Us feel safe.
Holding hands makes
Us feel close.
Holding hands makes
Us feel loved.
Holding hands makes
Us feel wanted.

Holding hands is really
Hand-hugging.
It is two hands
Hugging each other.

You don't have to
Hug a whole body,
Or hug a neck,
Or hug a shoulder,
Or hug a leg.
You can just
Hug a hand.

Hand-hugging
Is a favorite
Of husbands and wives,
Of some grandparents,
And of children and their
Parents.

The Bible tells us
That God is
So close to us
That it is as if
God were holding
Our hand.

You can't feel it
But God could be
Hand-hugging
With you
This very minute.

"But even so, you love me!" (Ps. 73:23)

Wrestling on the Floor

Can you answer riddles?
Try this one.
When is a hug not a hug?

A hug is not a hug
When you wrestle with
Your parents
On the floor.

Neither one of you says,
"Let's hug."
But as you wrestle

On the floor
You are really
Hugging each other.

Wrestling on the floor
Can be plenty of fun.
Sometimes your parents
Can hold you down
And sometimes
You can hold your parents
Down.

When you wrestle
On the floor,
You are really
Hugging each other.

Do you ever crawl
Across your mother's
Or your father's
Back?

Do you ever stand up
On your father's stomach?
Do you ever sit on his feet
And rock back and forth?

When you wrestle
On the floor,
You are really
Hugging each other.

Does your father ever
Lie on his back
And hold his arm
Straight up
And let you try to
Bend his arm down?

Do you ever try
To get away by
Crawling on
Your hands and knees?

Does your father
Reach out with one hand
And pull you back?

When you wrestle
On the floor,
You are really
Hugging each other.

"Let love guide your life." (Col. 3:14)

Kisses are Special

Have you ever thought
Of how many kinds of
Kisses there are?

There are wet kisses
Like babies give
That are messy.

There are short kisses
Like chicken pecks.

There are long kisses
That take forever.

There are kisses
On your forehead,
On your cheeks,
On your nose,
And on the
Lips.

There are
Good morning
Kisses.
There are
Good night
Kisses.

There are
I love you
Kisses
That fathers give to mothers.

There are kisses
That help sore fingers
Get better.

Kissing is like hugging,
But without using
Your arms.

When parents and
Children kiss,
They are saying
They love each other.

They are saying that
Everything is fine.

Kissing makes you
Feel loved.

Maybe that is why
The first Christians
Said "Hello"
By kissing.

**"Greet ye one another with an holy kiss."
(1 Cor. 16:20, KJV)**

Sitting Close

Robin is the kind of girl
Who likes to sit close.
She likes to snuggle up
Against her mother
On the couch
And be near her.

Robin's mother is gentle.
Robin's mother is pretty.
Robin's mother smells good.
Robin's mother knows a lot.
Robin's mother sings well.
Robin's mother reads with
A kind voice.

When Robin wants to
Sit close,
She gets one of her
Favorite books
And asks her mother
To read to her.

Those are some of
Robin's happiest times.
She sits close to
Her mother
And listens to
Her loving voice.

And Robin
Feels loved,
Sitting close.

"When you draw close to God, God will draw close to you." (James 4:8)

Do You Like to Frolic?

Do you like
to frolic?

Bears are great
Frolickers.

When they are young cubs,
Bears can often be seen
Pulling at each other
And tossing each other
Playfully.

The bears are frolicking.
This may be a new word
For you but
You probably already
Know how to frolic.

Bear cubs chase each other
And tumble over each other
And play games in the water.

The bears are careful
And almost never get hurt.
They just have a good time
Frolicking.

Adult people often like
To play with their children
The same way,

Either in the yard
Or on the floor.

It's fun to frolic
With a brother or sister
Or your parents.

**"Whatever you do, do it with kindness and
love." (1 Cor. 16:14)**

Help the Elderly

Do you ever visit people
In a nursing home?
Maybe they are old
And can't leave
Their rooms very often.

Or they might be sick
And they have been
Inside for a long time.

Sometimes we don't know
What to do
Or what to say
When we visit them.

The next time you visit
An older person
You could try
Holding his hand
For a few minutes.

Usually it makes him
Feel better if someone
Will hold his hand.

Most older people like
To have children around,
And when you touch
Their arms or hands,
Their days can go
A lot better.

When you talk to
An older person

And you put your hand
On his hand,
Look at his face.

See if your touch
Brings a smile to
An older person.

"You shall give due honor and respect to the elderly, in the fear of God." (Lev. 19:32)

Favorite Blanket

Did you ever have
A favorite blanket
Or a pillow that
You carried around?

If you did,
You enjoyed
The way it felt,
And its color,
And maybe a special
Corner of the blanket.

You might still have one
You like better than
Any other.

As a child grows older,
He stops carrying
A blanket.

After the blanket
Stays on the bed all the time,
He still has people
To hold.

Blankets are good to hold.
People are better to hold.

**"Enjoy other people and . . . like them, and
finally you will grow to love them deeply."
(2 Pet. 1:7)**

Swan-Back Ride

People are not the only ones
Who enjoy playing with
Their children.

Swans pick out one partner
(A husband or a wife)
And stay together all
Their lives.

When they have babies,
The young ones
Remain with their parents
For one year
Before they make
A home for themselves.

Both the mother
And the father
Share in taking care
Of their young ones.

Sometimes swan parents
Like to take
One of their children
For a piggyback ride.

The young swan
Will jump up
On Mother's back
Or Father's back
And ride
Around the lake.

Baby swans hold on
While safely riding
Between the swan's uplifted wings.

Some animals make
Good parents.

They keep their babies close
And care for them.

**"Most important of all, continue to show
deep love for each other, for love makes up
for many of your faults." (1 Pet. 4:8)**

No Thank You

Sometimes you just don't
Feel like being hugged.

You may not know why,
But today you don't want
Anyone to hug you.

Just tell the person
"No thank you"
And walk away.

You aren't being rude.
You are merely saying
How you feel
At the time.

And you are being
Polite,
If you tell him nicely.

No one needs to be hugged
When he doesn't feel like
Being hugged.

Your father's body belongs
To him.
Your mother's body belongs
To her.
And your body belongs
To you.

When you don't feel
Like being hugged,

Just tell the person
"No thank you,"
And walk away.

"A time not to hug." (Eccles. 3:5)

Leg-Hugging

When you are young,
It can be hard
To hug your mother
Or your father.

They stand up a lot
And they are *so tall*.

That must be
The reason
Children invented
Leg-hugging.

When it's done
Just right,
Leg-hugging
Can make
Everyone
Feel good.

A good
Leg-hug
Needs to be
Tight but also
Short.

If you leg-hug
For too long,
Your mother or
Father can't
Walk.

A leg-hug can be
A quiet hug

Because a hug
Is like speaking.

Before you leg-hug,
Always look up
To make sure
Your mother or father
Isn't carrying anything
That might spill
On you.

Leg-hugging
Is a good way
For a child
To say
"I love you."

"You should be like one big happy family, full of sympathy toward each other, loving one another with tender hearts and humble minds." (1 Pet. 3:8)

Baby Chipmunks

Have you ever seen
A baby chipmunk?

If you tried to see one
Just after it was born,
You would have to
Look closely.

A new baby chipmunk
Is only a little bit bigger
Than a bug.

Its eyes are tiny
And will not open
For a while.

There isn't much
Hair on its body
And it is
Red.

The mother chipmunk
Keeps her babies
In a hole in the ground
With grass and leaves.

It might be cold
And damp in their
New home,
But the mother chipmunk
Keeps them warm.

She snuggles her body
Up close to the babies

While she feeds them
Her milk.

It feels great
To have a mother
Who cares and
Likes to be close
To you.

**"Let him have all your worries and cares,
for he is always thinking about you and
watching everything that concerns you."
(1 Pet. 5:7)**

Strangers

Strangers can be
Very nice people
After you get to
Know them.

Strangers often
Become friends.
Then they aren't
Strangers anymore.

But a few strangers
Are *not* very nice.
You don't want to
Get to know them
At all.

At first you don't know
If a stranger is
A nice person or
Not a nice person.

That's why
We don't let strangers
Hug us.

Because we don't know
What they are like.

When you don't know someone,
You need to say no
If he tries to hug you.

You don't have to explain,
You don't have to argue,

All you have to do is
Say no.

You are big enough to say
No
When you need to.

**"Why . . . embrace . . . a stranger?"
(Prov. 5:20, KJV)**

Making It Better

When you bump your head
Against a table,
Or close a dresser drawer
On your finger,
Do you go and tell
Your mother or
Your father?

Do they kiss
Your finger or your head
Sometimes?

And then maybe
Your mother says,
"There, that will
Make it feel better."

Mothers are right.
Usually it does feel better
Because she kissed it.

It feels better because
Your mother touched it.

It feels better because
You know your mother
Loves you.

You can go back
To play
Because your mother
Is a good doctor.

**"I will comfort you . . . as a little one is
comforted by its mother." (Isa. 66:13)**

Touch Them Carefully

If you have a cactus plant,
You touch it carefully.

A cactus plant has
Sharp needles or thorns
To stop animals from
Eating the plant.

However, a few animals
Can get close and touch
A cactus if
They do it carefully.

Sometimes a brother
Or a sister
Or a parent feels bad
And he is grumpy.

He is like a
Sticky cactus and if
You want to get close,
You have to be
Very careful.

But if
You are gentle
And kind,
Sometimes
You can put
Your hand on
His shoulder

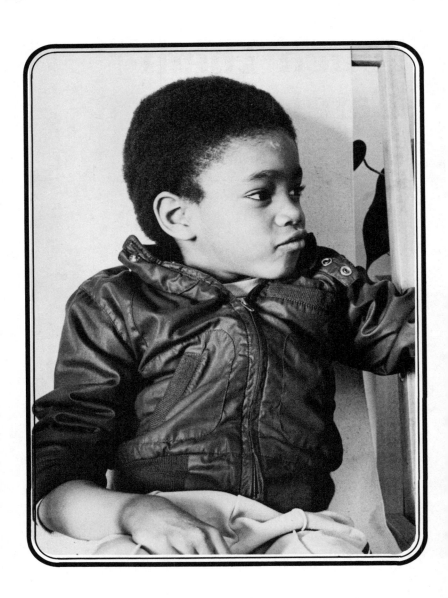

Without being
Sent away.

Often the grumpy person
Will turn and smile
Because he felt
Your touch on his shoulder.

If he tells you
To go away,
You should
Probably leave.

But sometimes you can
Reach between someone's cactus needles
And make him smile.

**"Be kind to each other, tenderhearted."
(Eph. 4:32)**

When a Koala Is Grumpy

One of the cutest animals
In the world
Is the koala
From Australia.

The first teddy bears
Were made to look like
The koala.
(But a koala isn't really a bear.)

A baby koala
Stays very close
To its mother
For the first year
Of its life.

During the first six months
The young koala
Rides in the pouch
On its mother's stomach.

By six months the koala becomes
Too big for the pouch
And climbs on its mother's
Back.

The cub rides for
The next six months
On its mother's back.

They stay close for one year
And hold on to each other
And feel loved
And wanted.

Sometimes the baby
Will get noisy
Or start acting badly.

When that happens,
The mother koala
Pulls the baby

Off her back
And places it
On her knee.

Then the mother
Spanks the baby.

The young koala
Yells and screams
And its mother
Places the baby
Up on her
Back.

Mothers like to see
Their children
Behave well.

"Discipline your son in his early years while there is hope. If you don't you will ruin his life." (Prov. 19:18)

Brushing Hair

A little girl said
That one of her
Happiest times is when
She brushes her
Father's hair.

He sits on the chair
And she stands
Behind him.

Her father sits still
And they talk about
Anything
While she brushes
His hair.

Sometimes she combs
His hair
In funny directions,
Or she might put
A pink barrette
In his hair.

Another happy time
Is when her mother
Or father
Brushes *her* hair.

It makes her feel clean.
It makes her feel pretty.
It makes her feel loved.

You don't have to spend money
Or travel half a day
To brush hair.
You don't have to
Send away for a package,
Or wait until summer
Or winter.

Brushing hair is easy.
Brushing hair is caring.
Brushing hair is gentle.
Brushing hair is love.

**"Let your good deeds glow for all to see, so
that they will praise your heavenly Father."
(Matt. 5:16)**

The Welcome-Home Hug

Some hugs are small
And quick.

Some hugs are half
And use only one shoulder.

Some hugs are bumpers.
You just bump
And move away.

But some hugs are
So important
And so big
And so happy,
They take all
You have.

When your brother
Or your sister
Or your mother
Or your father
Or your grandparents
Have been away
For a long time,
You want to give them
Your best
Welcome-home hug.

This hug squeezes tightly
And holds on until
The bottoms of your feet
Start to ache.

The welcome-home hug
Starts to take your
Breath away.

And when you are finished
You have to breathe hard
From the long hug.

Welcome-home hugs
Are special because

They make you feel great
To be together again.

And
Welcome-home hugs
Always make you
Smile.

"So he returned home to his father. And while he was still a long distance away, his father saw him coming, and was filled with loving pity and ran and embraced him and kissed him." (Luke 15:20)

The Jesus Touch

Jesus must have been
A warm, touching person.

He made a lot of
Sick people well.
Often when Jesus
Healed the sick
Person,
Jesus also touched
Him.

Jesus didn't have to
Touch a person
To make him well.

But Jesus touched
Him anyway.

It must have been
Special to have
Someone like Jesus
Touch him.

Jesus was gentle.
Jesus was caring.
Jesus was strong.
Jesus was kind.

Jesus knew it was
Important to have
Someone who loves you
Touch you.

You can feel love
In a person's touch.

**"Then he took her by the hand and called,
'Get up, little girl!' " (Luke 8:54)**

Happy Parents

Sea otters seem to have
A lot of fun
With their families.

They like to do things together
And show a lot of love
For each other.

Both the father and the mother
Like to be with their baby pups.

Sea otters usually have
One baby at a time.
And they do lots of things
With their pup.

If they have to travel
Over land,
The mother will carry
Her pup
In her mouth.

If they are swimming,
The mother will roll over
On her back
And let her pup
Sit on her stomach.

Parents and pups
Touch and hold
And hug a lot.

God gave them
A lot of love
For each other.

When it is time
To learn to swim,
The parent sea otter
Will watch carefully.

If the pup gets too tired,
Its parent will carry
It off quickly to the
Safe land.

Sea otters show
How much
They care for
Their young.

**"Love is very patient and kind."
(1 Cor. 13:4)**

Parents' Backs

Do you like to do
Special favors
For your parents?

Do you like to do
Things that make
Them happy?

At the end of
A long, hard day
Your parents might
Enjoy good, strong
Back rubs.

Sometimes it feels great
To have someone
Who loves you
Rub your back.

You could ask them
To lie on their
Stomachs
And tell them
To relax.

Then use your hands
To rub their backs
And shoulders.

Don't be surprised
If your father or mother
Purrs like a kitten.

That means he or she
Is happy.

And they love having
Someone they love
Rub their backs.

And you are someone
They really love.

"Let us stop just *saying* we love people; let us *really* love them, and *show it* by our *actions.*" (1 John 3:18)

Father-Climbing

Do you ever get the chance
To climb on your father?
It can be a lot of fun
For you
And your father.

He can sit on the floor
And you can climb
Up his back and
Maybe sit on his shoulders.

Or your father can lie
On his stomach
And you can roll over
His back.

Maybe you like to use
His back for a road
And play with your cars
Racing across his shoulders.

Chimpanzees like to do that, too.
Father chimps often lie
On the ground and let
Their offspring crawl
All over them.

While they play on top
Of their father,
He tickles his
Little chimps.

He will tickle them
Under the chin,

Or he will pat
Them on the head.

The little chimps like
To have male chimps
Around.

They are caring,
They are fun,
They are close.

God was good
To create fathers
Who care.

Grandmothers

How would you like
To make your grandmother
Feel special?

Climb up
On the couch
Sometime
And sit close
To your grandmother.

Not just close—
Sit extra close.

You don't have
To do anything.
You don't have
To say anything.
You don't have
To ask for anything.

Just sit close
To your grandmother
And *smile*.

See how long
It takes
For your grandmother
To smile back
At you.

Children are very good
At getting people
To smile.

And most of the time
Grandmothers smile easily
At their grandchildren.

**"White hair is a crown of glory."
(Prov. 16:31)**

Watching Parents

Have you ever watched
Your parents give
Each other a long,
Tight hug?

Does it make
You feel good
To see your parents
Hug?

Usually that means
Your parents are happy.

And when your parents
Are happy,
You are usually happy, too.

Some older children think
It is silly when their parents
Hug.

But it isn't silly.

Hugs are important
For two people
Who love each other.

Hugs mean your parents
Like to be together.

Hugs mean your parents
Like to have each other
Close.

Hugs mean your parents
Are smiling
Inside.

When you watch
Your parents hug,
You can feel
Very good
Inside.

It's fun to live
With parents who
Love each other.

**"Follow God's example in everything you
do just as a much loved child imitates his
father." (Eph. 5:1)**

Under His Wings

One of the best places
In the world
For a baby chick
Is underneath
Its mother's wings.

When a chick snuggles
Up under a wing
Of feathers,
Everything must seem fine.

It doesn't have to worry
About the cool wind
Or the darkness.

It feels safe and warm
Under mother hen's
Feathers.

Jesus told us He wanted us
To come to Him
In the same way
That a chick comes
To its mother.

Like a hen,
Jesus wants to
Put His arms
Around us and
Hold us close
To Him.

They aren't real wings,
And they aren't real arms;
They are better.

God reaches out
And wraps himself
Around us.

We can't feel Him
Or see Him,
But God is there
Holding us.

We can come to Jesus
And trust Him
Just as a chick
Trusts its mother.

"How often I have wanted to gather your children together as a hen gathers her chicks beneath her wings, but you wouldn't let me." (Matt. 23:37)

No-Touch Zones

If someone touches you
Behind your ears,
It might tickle.

If someone shakes
Your hand,
It feels friendly.

But there are some places
Where other people
Should not
Touch you.

We can call them
"No-touch zones."

These are the parts
Of your body
That are covered
When you wear
A bathing suit.

They are
"No-touch zones."

A few times
A doctor might
Need to touch you
At these places.

But other people
Should not touch
Your
"No-touch zones."

These parts of
Your body
Are special,
Are private.

If someone tried
To touch your
"No-touch zones,"
You should leave
And tell your
Parents
Right away.

God made your body
Special,
And He doesn't want
Other people
Touching your
"No-touch zones."

"We carefully protect from the eyes of others those parts [of our bodies] that should not be seen." (1 Cor. 12:23)

Not All the Time

Hugging is nice.
But if you hugged
All the time,
You couldn't eat.

Hugging is fine.
But if you hugged
All the time,
Mother couldn't
Wash clothes.

Hugging is good.
But if you hugged
All the time,
Who would fix
Supper?

Hugging is something
We do once in a while
And then we stop
And do something else.

No one wants
To hug
All the time.

**"Love is . . . never . . . selfish or rude.
Love does not demand its own way."
(1 Cor. 13:4, 5)**

Who Invented Hugs?

Do you ever wonder
Who invented hugs?

Maybe a scientist
Thought of it
And drew pictures
Of hugs
For people to follow.

Maybe a famous traveler
Saw people hugging
In the mountains
Of Tibet
And told everyone
About it.

Maybe a missionary
Saw a far-off
Tribe hugging
In the jungles
And told everyone
About it.

Maybe an animal trainer
Saw apes hugging
And he thought
He would try it
With his wife.

But hugging is
So helpful,
Hugging is
So nice.
Hugging is
So friendly.

Most likely
God
Invented hugging.

God likes to do
Good things
For us.

And hugging
Is very good.

"But whatever is good and perfect comes to us from God." (James 1:17)

Pets Are Special

Have you ever had a pet
That you liked to play with?
Maybe it was a dog
Or a cat or a horse.

Maybe your pet was a goat
Or a pig or a chicken.
Maybe your pet was a fish
Or a bird or a snake.

You like to name your pet,
Feed it and play games
With it.
Sometimes you even have to
Clean up for your pet.

It's also fun to hug your pet
As you carry it around
Or hold it in your lap.

(Unless it's a goldfish;
We shouldn't carry
Goldfish around.)

Sometimes a person can sit
For hours
And hold his pet
And talk to it.

He rubs the pet's neck
And runs his fingers
Through its fur.

And the pet might
Purr or coo
Because the pet is happy.

Many pets like to be held
Just as people like to be held.

Pets are special.
They are loving.
They like to be loved.
Pets are good to hold.

"If a person isn't loving and kind, it shows that he doesn't know God—for God is love." (1 John 4:8)

Washing Feet

During the time of Jesus,
Christians liked to show
Their love for each other
By washing each other's feet.

Some Christians today
Still wash
Each other's feet.

It is one way to show
That they care
About other people
And want to help them.

They soak the person's feet
With water
And then
Wipe them with
A towel.

Some Christians do it
Often
Because they want
To show their love
Often.

Jesus washed the feet
Of those
Who followed Him.
Jesus liked to show
His love for others.

"So he got up from the supper table, took off his robe, wrapped a towel around his loins, poured water into a basin, and began to wash the disciples' feet and to wipe them with the towel he had around him." (John 13:4, 5)

Skin Hunger

What do you do
When your body
Needs food?

You eat.

What do you do
If a plant
Needs water?

You water it.

What do you do
If your car
Needs a wash?

You wash it.

What do you do
When your skin
Needs food?

When you need
Someone's hand
On yours
Or an arm
Around your
Shoulder?
You go to your parents
And you hold them.

Then your skin gets
The touch it needs

And your parents get
The touch they need.

Hair needs
To be combed.

Teeth need
To be brushed.

A sore spot needs
To be cared for.

And skin needs
To be touched.

That is one
Of the reasons
God gave us parents.

**"Love each other with brotherly affection."
(Rom. 12:10)**

Hugging Porcupines

Have you ever thought
About how hard
It would be to
Hug a porcupine?

A porcupine's back
Has long, sharp needles
All over it.
The needles are called
Quills.

A porcupine may have
30,000 quills
All over its body.

If a porcupine
Swings its tail,
An enemy could soon
Have his leg
Filled with quills.

But once in a while
A porcupine needs a hug.

Porcupines can
Hug each other.
If they are careful,
Two porcupines will
Hug each other
Belly to belly.

Porcupine babies hug.
And their parents hug,
Even if they
Are filled
With quills.

Everybody needs a hug—
Even porcupines.

**"My prayer for you is that you will overflow
more and more with love for others."
(Phil. 1:9)**

Hugging Jesus

Have you ever seen
Two men hug?
Maybe they hadn't
Seen each other
In a long time.

Or maybe they had won
A baseball game
And they were so happy
They jumped
Into each other's arms
And squeezed each other.

Some men don't like to hug,
But others grab each other
With gigantic bear hugs.

Jesus and His men friends
Worked together for three years.
They faced danger together.
They fed people together.
They healed the sick together.
They preached about God together.

They had many happy times.
They had many sad times.

One time when Jesus
And His friends
Were eating together,
One of His friends
Put his head on
Jesus' chest.

They were close.
They were caring.

And they liked
Working together.

It feels good
To know
That someone
Cares
About you.

**"Now there was leaning on Jesus' bosom
one of his disciples, whom Jesus loved."
(John 13:23, KJV)**

A Calm Hug

Have you ever watched
A scary show
On television?

Did it make you
Afraid and lonely?

It sounds like
You needed
A calm hug.

Sometimes these hugs
Feel the best of all.
They make you feel
Like everything
Will be fine.

Have you ever been
Frightened
By a barking dog?

Did you run
Inside the house?
Were you excited
And maybe shaking?

It sounds like
You needed
A calm hug.

Parents are good
At giving
Calm hugs.

Grandparents are
Excellent at giving
Calm hugs.

Some brothers and sisters
Can give
A perfect calm hug.

All of us need them
Sometimes.
Even parents become
Upset
And need
A calm hug.

It feels great
To get one.
It's even better
To give
A calm hug.

"Be full of love for others, following the example of Christ who loved you and gave himself to God as a sacrifice to take away your sins." (Eph. 5:2)

Being Tucked In

One of the best times
For children
And for parents is
When children get
Tucked in at night.

It's a good time
To tell stories
Or ask questions
About what happened
During the day.

This is also a good time
To be close
And know someone cares.

If you could watch
Baby cottontail rabbits,
You might see the mother
Tuck her babies in.

After they have finished
Eating,
The babies lie down
And go to sleep.

As they start to doze off,
Their mother covers them
With leaves and fur
And grass.

The baby rabbits curl up
With each other
And go to sleep.

It's nice to have
Someone to tuck
You in.

Are You Ticklish?

If someone wanted
To make you laugh,
Where are you
The most ticklish?

When someone tickles
You on the side,
Does that make you
Laugh and wiggle?

What if someone
Tickles your
Neck?

Does that make you
Bend over
And giggle?

What about
The bottoms
Of your feet?

Some people
Can't stand
To have their feet
Tickled.

It makes them
Laugh so hard,
It begins to hurt.

That is why
We don't tickle
For too long.

We don't want
To make anyone hurt.

But sometimes
It feels great
To tickle
And to be
Tickled.

Where is your
Favorite place
To be tickled,
Or
Would you
Rather keep it
A secret?

"A time to laugh." (Eccles. 3:4)

Jesus Holds Children

Jesus enjoyed having
Little children
Near Him.

He liked to talk
To children.
And when they
Were sick,
He often made
Them well.

Sometimes Jesus would
Pick up children
And hold them.

Jesus wanted children
To know that
God was their
Heavenly Father
And that God
Loves children.

Some people
Don't want
Children around.

They chase them away
And want to be
Alone.

Jesus liked to see
Children
And be with them,
And pick them up,
And hold them.

Jesus has a great love
For children.

**"Then he took the children into his arms
and placed his hands on their heads and
he blessed them." (Mark 10:16)**

What Is Nuzzling?

Sometimes when your
Father is asleep
On the couch,
Do you climb up
And lie close to him?

And sometimes do you
Fall asleep
Next to him?

If you do,
You know how to
Nuzzle.

Other times you don't
Go to sleep,
But you just lie still
And be real quiet.

You do that because
It is fun to
Nuzzle
With your parents.

You know you
Really love someone
When you nuzzle with them.

Fawns are young deer
And they like to

Nuzzle
With their mother,
The doe.

When they are first born,
Fawns have trouble walking
And taking care of themselves,
So they nuzzle a lot.

Parents like to nuzzle, too.
Sometimes when you are asleep
On the couch
Or early at night,
Your mother or father will
Lie next to you and
Nuzzle,
Because they think
You are special.

Nuzzling
Makes you
Feel special.

"Dear friends, let us practice loving each other, for love comes from God and those who are loving and kind show that they are the children of God." (1 John 4:7)

The Stiff Hug

Have you ever watched
Two people hug when
They don't know each other
Very well?

They use a stiff hug.
They don't really
Reach for each other.

Watch sometime.
They bend at the waist
And sort of give
A neck hug.

Their arms barely
Touch each other
And they act
Afraid that
They might
Get too close.

They look a little bit
Like toy soldiers
Leaning against each other.

Maybe when they
Get to know each other
Better,
They will learn to
Hug each other
Better.

"Don't just pretend that you love others: really love them." (Rom. 12:9)

Horseback Riding

June liked
To ride horseback
In her living room.

She didn't have
A real horse,
But her father
Was willing
To be her horse.

Her father would
Get down
On his hands and knees,
And June would
Climb up
On her father's back.

Her father would
Walk around
On his hands and knees
And June would ride
On top
Of her father's back.

June would hold on
To the back
Of her father's shirt
So she wouldn't
Fall off.

Sometimes her father
Would wiggle from
Side to side
Or hurry
Across the floor.

And June would
Hold on tightly.

And she would
Laugh and giggle.

It was fun
To be close
To her father.

And
It was fun
For her father
To be close
To June.

**"A child's pride is her father."
(Prov. 17:6, author's paraphrase)**

How to Hug a Cat

When you hug a cat,
Hold it gently in one arm
And pet it with your
Other hand.

Usually a happy cat
Will purr
When you hold it.

But a cat will
Not purr
If you squeeze it tightly
Around the stomach.

And a cat will
Not purr
If you hug its neck
Until its eyes
Become large.

And a cat will
Not purr
If you hug it upside down
And its tail hits
You in the face.

When you hug a cat,
Hold it gently in one arm
And pet it with your
Other hand.

Usually a happy cat
Will purr when you
Hold it.

"Love is very patient and kind."
(1 Cor. 13:4)

Grandfather's Knee

It's nice to have
Special places.

When you sit close
To your mother
On the couch,
That's a special place.

When you get to
Ride on
Your father's back,
That's a special place.

But one of the most
Special places
In the world
Is sitting
On your grandfather's knee.

Grandfathers aren't like
Other people.
They have been around
A long time.

Grandfathers
Know stories
That no one else
Seems to know.

And grandfathers
Often know tricks

That make their
Grandchildren laugh
And want to be
Near them.

Grandfathers
Like little children.
And a grandfather likes
To have children
Climb up on his lap.

And when a grandchild
Gets sleepy, he can
Snuggle up into his
Grandfather's arms
And go to sleep.

Grandfathers like that.

There is no place
More special than
Sitting on a grandfather's
Knee.

**"An old man's grandchildren are his
crowning glory." (Prov. 17:6)**

Asleep in His Arms

Have you ever climbed up
Into your father's arms
When you felt tired?

You wanted to be close
To someone,
So you leaned
Against your father's chest.

And it felt good
To be close
To someone you love.

Soon you found yourself
Putting your head
On his shoulder.

And your eyes kept
Closing because
You were getting
Sleepy.

And it felt good
To be close
To someone you love.

Before long,
You were
Asleep
And breathing deeply
And feeling peaceful.

And your father
Felt good, too,
Because he knows
You love him.

It feels good
To fall asleep
In your father's arms.